EUPHO

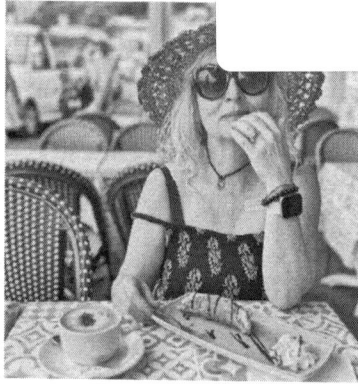

Melanie Neads is a poet, playwright and dramaturge from Salford whose poetry collection with Sarah Miller was Best Collaborative Work runner-up at the Saboteur Awards. Her plays have won the Forever Manchester Award, been short-listed for the Shelagh Delaney Award, and performed on radio by victims of youth crime for Live from Worktown's Standing Together community safety project. Melanie co-founded the Pavilion Theatre Company in Bolton, was Drama Co-ordinator for Salford Young People's University, and is a tantric and somatic yoga teacher, and award-winning English and Drama SEN teacher. She has taught and lived in Australia, India, Poland, Israel and the USA – experiences which infuse her work.

Also by the author

Selkie Singing at the Passing Place
(with Sarah Miller)

MANCHESTER
A UNESCO City
of Literature

northern
fiction
alliance

MELANIE NEADS
EUPHORIA

Flapjack Press

flapjackpress.co.uk
Exploring the synergy between performance and the page

Published in 2024 by Flapjack Press
Salford, Gtr Manchester
⊕ flapjackpress.co.uk · ▶ flapjackpress2520
f Flapjack Press · 𝕏 FlapjackPress

ISBN 978-1-0686052-1-5

© melanie_neads · © ywellbeingwarriors

Printed by Imprint Digital
Exeter, Devon
⊕ imprintdigital.com

FSC

*Dedicated to
all the survivors,
misfits and elves.*

CONTENTS

Hello survivors, misfits and elves, how are you? Would you mind doing me a favour and take a long inhalation through the nose? Hold. Hold ... and breathe out. Doesn't that feel better?

Firstly, thank you for buying *Euphoria* and I Brownie-Girl-Promise that any royalties will be spent on ridiculous items, such as snorkels, sherbet and adventure. I decided to write an 'Introduction' as I wanted to meet you and tell you about the rationale behind writing this book.

I first met univocal poetry when I heard the lovely Rob Steventon (buy his book too![1]) read a poem at Manchester Central Library. I was mesmerised by the playfulness of his poem, and as a yoga teacher and special needs teacher I'm all about the play. The earliest known use of univocalics was in the mid-1500s. But I'm digressing. You will notice I do that, but it's the way my brain's wired. So, play: Before I had heard Rob's poem, I was visiting the Tate in London and, in a nearby second-hand bookshop, found a book on brain training activities, many of which I've since incorporated into my lesson plans as starters or settlers. I found that students of all ages loved it, with my own favourite being *draw something with your non-dominant hand* (see p.42). It's supposed to strengthen cognitive skills in a fun and accessible way, and it can help break down barriers to learning. I can't draw (see p.42), and my art teacher used to send me to water the plants rather than have me cry for an hour when asked to, but I didn't mind doing this activity because *non-dominant hand* is a level playing field and is meant to balance out my creative brain. Make me more logical or something.

Anyway, two years ago I had a TIA (aka a mini-stroke) and although the symptoms pass quickly, I was left with severe anxiety. The hospital (go NHS!) provided me with a brain training manual which I would recommend to anyone, whether it be wordsearches, Wordle or Sudoku. But, not being logic-minded, Sudoku fell flat with me, so my husband suggested univocal poems and thus the monster was created.

I started with political poems, as Trump, BoJo, Rishi and Truss were univocal names and ripe for satire. I performed as 'Madame O' with a patch over one eye, as you do. But then I challenged myself to write about societal issues, such as Gaza, domestic abuse, and cuts to the creative arts sector. Although univocalics do lend themselves to the silly, such as the plight of owls (again, see p.42).

Abracadabra … here come the instructions to write your own univocal poem. But – ✳warning✳ – it can be addictive.

Firstly, decide on your vowel. Personally, I'd avoid 'U' as it's just plain obstinate. Then, think of all the univocal words which use only that vowel (you can use this book to help you), and whilst you're writing or typing them an idea will come. If it doesn't, read or listen to the News. Start your poem, and if you are getting exasperated thinking *I want to say this* then a good old fashioned Thesaurus will be your best friend. National Poetry Writing Month (NaPoWriMo) is a good source of poetry prompts – this year I managed a univocal poem for each one.

I've made my own univocal dictionary and this travels everywhere with me; on the bus, to work, to the shops, even on holiday. If you hear univocal words write them down. Think outside the box. You might annoy people on your univocal journey, trip, expedition, trek, voyage and tour, but *you* be *you* because you are perfectly velveteen.

Melanie Neads
July 2024

---

[1] *How I Made My Millions* by Rob Steventon [Flapjack Press, 2021].

Euphoria. Noun.
State of intense excitement.
Contains all vowels.

Gene Gets Gender

Gene gets gender,
yet gender perplexes,
vexes repressed men.
They see gender pre-set –
the secret sex between the legs.
Flesh be gender,
gender be flesh.

Gene feels he's she, her, them.
Repressed men sneer, jeer; perverse.
Reject Gene's preferred self.
He never ever be she,
she never ever be he.
Yet Gene feels she's French temptress,
pens fervent femme verse –
Je te presente ...

Meets the streets.
Red dress, heels, new beret,
strength,
free speech.

Beefy beerbelly men mêlée.
Flesh be gender,
gender be flesh.
He never ever she,
she never ever he.

Gender breezes serenely,
even when repressed men sneer; perverse.

He-she-them-they
merely letters we select.
Reject, reject!
Flesh be gender,
gender be flesh.
Bend gender, be.
Perfect, perfect, perfectly be.
Gene gets gender.

SPRING HYMN

It is.
It is still wintry.

Spring limps in with misty ill will,
with whirling winds flinging chill,
with hissy fits spitting.
It is. It is.

Sing Spring in with high hymns,
sing Spring in with kind hymns,
sing inspiring hymns,
sing hymns inviting in light nights

'til Spring is girlish,
'til Spring is impish,
'til lily lifts with mirth,
'til bliss sighs in birth.

Sing, sing, sing.
It is.
It is Spring.

Let Me Be Green Cypress Tree

Let me be green Cypress tree,
evergreen, ever seen, ever resplendent.
Let me be never ever meek,
yet never self-centred,
perfectly myself,
seeded,
weeded,
scented,
effervescently dressed.

Blend me.
Let me be Cypress tree;
mend,
remedy.
Let me lessen stress,
prevent wheezes,
sneezes.

Let me be Cypress tree.
Let me be needed.

Gaza Ghazal

Ya Allah, man, a small anthrax ant and all.
Gaza at war as many stars fall.

A fat-cat cash war that Gaza can't pay.
Abraham slays Abraham as stars fall.

A camp baby crawls past tanks.
A fatal blast. Last gasp as stars fall.

Dawns and days as dark as Shaytan's black abyss.
Sandbags stand tall as stars fall.

Alas, alack, alarm! Army attacks farmlands.
A haggard Gaza wants maps back. Stars fall.

BoJo

So long BoJo, so long kooky clown!
So long dodgy moron.
Blood moon's howls
stop clown show.
Top job not for clown now.
Polls don't root for BoJo now.
No to clown, no to BoJo.

No, no, no BoJo, words won't work.
Words, lots of strong words.
Oh golly gosh! Lots of goofs,
lots of soft showy shots.

Oopsy boopsy, no comfort for poor
or old or cold torsos on floor.
Sorry no comfort for symptoms of pox,
months of loss, of low, of lockdown,
of worry on worry on worry.

How now, brown cow?
How now?

No lockdown for Old London Town,
nor for downtown Soho or BoJo.

So long clown, so long.
No Zoom for poor folks.
No chlorophyll cocoons.

Lockdown only for who do Lotto,
poor folks, old folks, snowdrops
down, down on rock bottom.

So long clown, so long.
Don't stop for photoshoots or promos.
No good now.
Forgo protocol – too slow.

Stop clown show.
Don't go tomorrow.
Not two o'clock. Go now.
Now!

Oh bollocks
bollocks
  bollocks
   bollocks
    bollocks
     bollocks
      bollocks
       bollocks
        bollocks

VIXI, VIDI, VICI, VINI
(I lived, I saw, I won, I drank wine)

Rishi wins tipsy twilight-till-midnight kingship p^{is}s$_i$$_n$$_g$ fight.

King Rishi's big dick
wins with right wing swing.
Rishi is king. King Rishi is giddy.
Thinks it's simply spiffing.

Critics fifty-fifty.
First instincts grim.
Misgivings.

Rishi is bit shifty, bit drippy, bit dim.
His grim mimicry:
"Vixi, vidi, vici, vini.

King is my birthright.
Pissing is my birthright!"

This ship will split.
With hindsight,
Rishi is slick rich prick,
bit sick in mind.

Brits in crisis;
Rishi's lip-kiss is cryptic.
This ship is sinking.
King Rishi thinks *winning,*
I'm winning.

Big fish in tiny sink.
Tiny fish swimming in inky linns.

Rishi drifting in his flimsy dinghy
with high winds, spinning,
spinning.

Lightning hits.
Shit.
Ship in bits.
Sinking, sinking.
Dying, dying.

King Rishi drinks pink Pimms in dinghy
whilst Brits' ship is sinking.
Sinks.

Vixi, vidi, vici, vini!

HOWL
(New York School Poem[2])

Oh God. Oh God. Oh Hollow Crown.
Sorry for loss of words. Howl! Forgot words. Forgot words.
Yoko Ono's songs no comfort now.
Don't worry, don't worry, only for Kyoko.

Snoop Dog got blow from cool cop.
J-Lo got crotch spots 'n' mono from Hollywood Bowl show.
Mythology of Hollywood. Howl.
Howl. God don't know, God don't know. How?

God don't know Don. Don don't know God. Howl.
Symphony of dystrophy.
Poor folks loot shops:
tools, tongs, spoons, stools, clocks, food.
Stop!
Don't shoot, don't shoot folks of color!
Two shots shook world.
Howl!

God nor Don no comfort for poor
(God won't stop wolf from door).
Howl. Howl. No God, no God!

Don owns world, owns shops, owns schools, owns ports,
owns porn, owns stocks, owns bookshops, owns bombs.
God for posh boys, not for poor.
Monsoons on poor.

Bolts doors of Oronoco.
Bolts doors of Boston.
Bolts doors of Stony Brook.
Noon.
Two dogs growl *soon, soon.*
Blood moon of sorrow.

Tomorrow?
Don got condom on. Knock. Knock.
Clowns show of cock. Oh God. Oh God.
Stop, God, stop!
Snowdrops bloom on lost world.
Forty photos of tombs.
World's womb blown to Mordor.
Woodstock cooks.
Too hot, God, too hot.

Not good, God, not good.
Howl. Howl.

---

[2] The Rules: i. At least one addressee (to which you may or may not wish to dedicate your poem); ii. Use of specific place names and dates (time, day, month, year) – especially the names of places in and around New York City; iii. Prolific use of proper names; iv. At least one reminiscence, aside, digression or anecdote; v. One or more quotations, especially from things people have said in conversation or through the media; vi. A moment where you call into question at least one thing you have said or proposed throughout your poem so far; vii. Something that sounds amazing even if it doesn't make any sense to you; viii. Pop cultural references; ix. Consumer goods/services; x. Mention of natural phenomena (in which natural phenomena do not appear 'natural').

Eggshell Green

She's depressed.
Her self-esteem's eggshell.
She feels she's less,
feels herself messy,
feels feeble,
feels defenceless.
She's depressed.

Her sphere:
the edge.

She's depressed.
Stressed, she never expresses her needs;
she resents help.
The green seeds: mercy.
She pretends she's well.
She tells the senseless few she's deeply self.
Secretly,
she seeks the end.

She's sleepless,
wrestles the wretched sheep between the sheets,
begs them, *"Let me sleep, let me sleep."*
Stressed shepherdess.

She's depressed, needs rest.
Tender sleep.
Herself reset.
Herself mended.
Herself better.

Yet, her self-esteem's eggshell.

TO DO OR NOT TO DO

Poor Tom knows not – to do or not to do.
Tom doth sorrow-sob; poor boy, so forlorn.
Tom doth look from top to bottom – for who?
For goodly Crow, who of two phlox moons born.

Crow's consort of gorgons, of gods, of ghosts.
Nonny no! Tom doth not know of Crow's worth
so doth not woo. Bold. Bow down lowly host.
Horror. No Crow's voodoo, only hold forth!

Cold snowstorms do blow. Oh! Cross Crow doth scold.
Now, fool-Tom to go from not know to gloom,
Not to nor from. Poltroon to worm food-fold,
hot blood to rot. No tomorrow. Tom's doom.

Forsooth, good folks! To know or not to know?
Hold soft, hold slow words of most holy Crow.

TYWNDYLLNGS

"Why myrrh?
Why myrrh?"
my kynd cry, cry.

Shy hymns by Byrls,
sly hymns by Byrls;
"Pyx, pyx."

"Why myrrh?
Why myrrh?"
hywl my kynd,
my kynd.

Crypt myth,
crypt myth.
"Shhhh, tywndyllngs."

RESENTMENT

Resentment sleeps deeply.
Keeps secrets.

Resentment's clever.

Never ever tells
where felled men wept.

       Mercy. Mercy.

Never tells
where felled men bled
                severed flesh.
Never tells
where felled men rest, sleep deep.

The helmeted Elm
keeps resentment's secrets.
Even when the relentless wren beseeches
"Where, where?"
the Elm tree keeps serene.
Gentle breeze weeps
"Mercy, mercy."

Resentment sleeps deep.
Keeps secrets.
Never ever tells.

BARD

Adam basks at bar. A brandy glass at hand. Adam's a man as alpha as Atlas. Ava walks past – all scarf and black, sparkly hat. Fragrant as a March pansy at dawn.

ADAM

Yass slay!

BARD

Adam grabs at Ava's arm.

AVA

What? Away, away!

BARD

Ava gasps.

ADAM

M'lady.

BARD

Adam pats Ava's arm and flaps a wax flag.

ADAM

Adam.

BARD

Ava calms and has warmth.

AVA

Ava.

BARD

Adam and Ava's hands clasp. At last. At last. Adam and Ava cast as happy larks. A play, a happy ballad sang by bards.

ADAM

Wanna brandy?

AVA

Nah thanks, Adam.

ADAM

Schnapps?

AVA

Nah.

ADAM

Wanna play cards ... Snap?

AVA

Hardly!

ADAM

Fancy a sassy snapchat snap?

BARD

Ava gags.

AVA

What ya say?

ADAM

Lady-parts snapchat? ... Bang, bang.

AVA

Lady-parts? ... Nah thanks, a man that chats that fast can't
last.

BARD

Ava wags hand.

ADAM

Calm, man has zany bants ...

BARD

Ava's hand falls away. Adam and Ava sway apart. A vast chasm as bar war starts.

AVA

Watch ya brandy chat, ya ass!

ADAM

My ass as hard as brass.

AVA

Ya what? … Ya say ya ass as hard as brass … Ya ass as hard as a bad banana … Ya all brawn, Adam, nah smarts.

ADAM

Slag!

AVA

Ya what?

ADAM

Ha ha, hashtag bants!

BARD

Ava rants.

AVA

Bants? Bants?

ADAM

Man wants bants.

AVA

A lad wants bants.

ADAM

Bants baby … Sarcasm.

AVA

Call that sarcasm, Adam?

ADAM

Adam has swag. Fact!

AVA

Nah sway man. Adam's a lad.

ADAM

A lad? ... Ada's cray, cray.

AVA

Cray, cray? ... Back way away Stan!

BARD

Adam sways back.

ADAM

Bants, bants, baby.

AVA

Ya bants as awkward as my grandma's asthma.

ADAM

Rah! ... Adam a marksman, Ava.

AVA

What?

ADAM

Bang, bang.

AVA

Adam's daft.

BARD

Adam's aghast.

ADAM

Calm, calm.

AVA

Harm, harm.

BARD

Ava's antsy. Claws sharp.

ADAM

Ah, ya salty gyal.

AVA

Salty! Call that charm, Adam?

ADAM

Ah, charm … Man can charm … Ava's as salty as sand.

AVA

Sand?

ADAM

Ya. Alaskan sand, baby.

AVA

Alaska? What?

ADAM

Ava as stark as Alaskan sand.

AVA

Adam, ya trashy bastard.

ADAM

Fat slag!

BARD

Ava clasps at handbag strap and stands. A land far, far away.

ADAM

Stay.

AVA

Nah way.

ADAM

Stay.

BARD

Ava yawns.

ADAM

Stay.

AVA

Hashtag spam.

BARD

Ava flaps tan flag and walks away. Adam's a man as alpha
as Atlas ... Alas, Atlas lacks class and bants.

COWBOYS

Cowboys don't do condoms
for bonks, blowjobs or romcoms.

Cowboys do not smoothly woo.
No soft words or song of who.
Only long loops of *whoop, whoop!*
Only poxy, moxy-dropsy droop.

Don't do cowboys or romcoms.
Do condoms.

JUMP, HUMPTY, JUMP!

Humpty Dumpty up.
Humpty Dumpty punchdrunk.

Ugly duck spurs:
"Jump, Humpty, jump!"

Humpty Dumpty jumps.
Bumpty thump, bump, bump.

Humpty Dumpty sunny tum up.
Ugly duck's smug.

KAKALAKA

Frantz Kafka had angst.
Phantasmal and smart,
Frantz Kafka had a hard start.
Sad Kafka.

Kafka's papa was a wall,
Kafka's mama was a shawl,
a shawl that lacks warmth.
Sad Kafka.

As a lad, Kafka saw many wars.
Ghastly grand plans blast faraway lands;
as kalt as glass,
as kalt as papa.

Sad Kafka drank
dank, dark, Asbach brandy.

Sad Frantz Kafka had many hats.
A harsh law cap,
a Panama hat,
a Gamsbart,
a Kafka hard hat.

Kafka was a bard,
calls all angst art.
Kafka's art was fantasy;
had a dark charm
and sarcasm that had snap,
a clap back at papa and past.

Samsa was Kafka,
Kafka was Samsa.

A kakalaka
that crawls walls,
that falls away, small.

All and all,
Kafka was sad.
A kakalaka.

GREEK

There were three feckless sellers ere Greece.
Elder Ell, well, he sells, he sells hell – hens' teeth;
Eryx sells sex, relentlessly zesty sex, then weeps;
the shepherd Hermes breeds three-legged, sleepy sheep.
Yet, best bet's Estes: she keeps esteemed fleece.

BUNTY

Bunty hunts Chuck, Buck, Butch, Rufus, Gus.
Buck sucks thumb; *mummy, mummy, mum.*
Busty Bunty grunts, shunts Buck. Cush; crush.

Bunty's just lustful, mustn't fuss, shush, shush.
Bunty guts, cuts up Butch. Susurrus hums.
Butch's skull just slurry; slushy mush.

Bunty hunts Chuck, Rufus, Gus.
Drugs: dun. Rufus: numb. Rufus: succumbs.
Bunty's hungry; Rufus's just rush-grub, but lush.

Bunty hunts Chuck, Gus.
Gus, lunk-stun, but must run, run.
Bunty snuffs Gus; Gus-bury-bush.

Bunty's just lustful, mustn't fuss, shush, shush.
Shut up, just shut up Bunty! Chuck pulls gun.
But unlucky, plucky Chuck.
                              Bunty's succubus.

Bunty hunts Chuck, Buck, Butch, Rufus, Gus ... Us.
Succubus uprush, just lustful, mustn't fuss, shush, shush.

SHAMBALA BANANA

Sally's (Harvard Grad) shaman stands
as bland and as gassy as Canada.

Shaman claps hands,
chants madcap mantra.

Shambhala Banana, Shambhala Banana,
Shambhala Banana, Shambhala Banana.

Shaman's as mad as Mahabharata saga.
"That man's a scam, bad, bad karma," says Sally calmly.

Clan backs away awkwardly.
Shambala Banana, Shambala Banana.

HUNGRY MUCH?

Pub grub
Bull's rump
Skunk curry
Slug's slurry
Muck pup mush

✳ ✳

Bugs Bunny's bumfluff
Sulphur burps
Hummus pulp
Mums' hurtful slurs
Mundungus

✳ ✳

Full-crust crunchy buns
Munchy Curly Wurly curds
Mucky husky puppy's fur
Smurf 'n' turf
Chunks

✳ ✳

Plum puds
Lumpy nut fungus
Musty butt-plugs
Lusty ▇▇▇ *gushy* ▇▇▇ [3]
Yummy yum

---

[3] Redacted on psychological and moral welfare grounds, as well as taste. The Editor would like to make the following statement: ▇▇ ▇▇▇▇ ▇▇▇ ▇▇ ▇▇ ▇▇. ▇▇▇▇. ▇▇▇▇▇. ▇▇▇▇▇ ▇▇▇ ▇▇. ▇▇ ▇▇▇▇

HORNY OWLS

Noon o'clock too soon
for 'whoo' hoots from horny owls.
Look to moon to woo.

[qv p.8: Here's Otto the Horny Owl, a brain training
example of *draw something with your non-dominant hand.*]

VELVETEEN

The scene's set.
Celeste greets Evelyn.

CELESTE
Hey there serf!

EVELYN
Me?

CELESTE
Yes, thee.

EVELYN
Thee?

CELESTE
Yes, let's pretend – we're velveteen?

EVELYN
Never!

CELESTE
Be genteel velveteen.

EVELYN
Never.

CELESTE
Every velveteen pretender gets presents.

EVELYN
Presents?

CELESTE
Pretty jewellery.

EVELYN
Well then ... Me be thee!

CELESTE
Greet me, reverently.

EVELYN
(Evelyn kneels)
Evelyn.

CELESTE
Where's the sheep, Evelyn?

EVELYN
Erm ... Sheep?

CELESTE
Thee be shepherdess?

EVELYN
Erm ... Erm ...

CELESTE
Pretty jewellery, Evelyn ...

EVELYN
Well then, me be shepherdess.

CELESTE
Be thee green, Evelyn?

EVELYN
Green?

CELESTE
Yes green, Evelyn.

EVELYN
Erm ...

CELESTE
Very pretty jewellery ...

EVELYN
Erm ... Well, yes then.

CELESTE
The trees need help, Evelyn.

EVELYN
Help?

CELESTE
Yes, even the Cherry trees need help.

EVELYN
Cherry trees?

CELESTE
Yes.

EVELYN
Well, yes then.

CELESTE
Yes?

EVELYN
Yes.

CELESTE
Tell the trees.

EVELYN
Tell them?

CELESTE
Tell the trees secrets.

EVELYN

Secrets?

CELESTE

Deep, sleepy, serene secrets.

EVELYN

Erm …

CELESTE

Tell them between-the-sheets secrets, Evelyn.

EVELYN

Seems extreme.

CELESTE

Be sweet, be gentle, be green, Evelyn.

EVELYN

Erm …

CELESTE

Tell the trees. Tell the trees, Evelyn.

EVELYN

She wrestles me between the sheets … Relentless
tenderness …

CELESTE

She?

EVELYN

Yes, she.

CELESTE

Very velveteen …

EVELYN

Be the Cherry trees cheered?

CELESTE
The Cherry trees weep.

EVELYN
Weep?

CELESTE
Perfect newness.

EVELYN
The end? Evelyn be free?

CELESTE
Never ends.

EVELYN
Evelyn be free?

CELESTE
Yes, when she meets me by the trees.

EVELYN
Never.

CELESTE
Evelyn, be sweet, be gentle.

EVELYN
Never ever.

CELESTE
Be bejewelled velveteen she, Evelyn.

EVELYN
Celeste see the jewels then?

CELESTE
Meet me, then jewels, Evelyn.

EVELYN
Jewels, then Evelyn meet thee.

CELESTE
Well … Erm … Yes, then … Here.

EVELYN
(Evelyn tests the jewels between her teeth)
Pretty, pretty …
(Evelyn screeches)

CELESTE
Yes, Evelyn?

EVELYN
These jewels effete!

CELESTE
Yes.

EVELYN
Pretend jewels!

CELESTE
Yes.

EVELYN
Then thee be the velveteen pretender!

CELESTE
Yes … Thee be green, Evelyn, thee be green.

TLDR

SC WYD

FB TDTM

SC WTF

FB JK

SC BRB

FB K

SC ...

FB FFS

SC BK NW

SC BTW HBD

FB TX

FB TDTM

SC WTF

FB JK NBD

SC RLY

FB TBH

SC LMK

FB TDTM PLS

SC GTG

FB Y

SC YHBT

NEWS GEEK
(Fill in as you feel appropriate)

Experts ▮ secret trend ▮ celeb chefs ▮ sexy ▮

Essex ▮ speechless ▮ her left leg ▮ ▮ Ely

Peter Sellers ▮

▮ ▮ bees end ▮ event

Get set, ▮ ▮ *Peter* presenter

Perfect egg ▮ best kept ▮ ▮

▮ screeched helplessly ▮ glen ▮ ▮ defence

Detente ▮ ▮ Egypt ▮ ▮

Elk ▮ deer greet ▮ ▮ ▮ street

Welsh whelks ▮ leeks ▮ ▮ fête

Seedy Ken ▮ ▮ ▮ Severn Trent sewer

Celery lessens ▮ ▮

French men ▮ smelly cheese ▮

Better sex ▮ jelly blended ▮ ▮

Best dressed celeb ▮ The Met's red ▮ ▮ ▮ Dee

Severe ▮ sever ▮ ▮ New Jersey

Feel stressed? Then ▮ ▮ ▮ ▮

JAZZ MAN JACK

Jazz man Jack,
crazy cat,
jazz my bag baby.
An ass man,
a half glass man,
as sharp as a tack.
Jack plays sax;
Manhattan bar,
fat-cats and vamps.
Jazz man Jack
sang a standard track,
shady lady and skat man
razzmatazz
and all that jazz.

U.S.

Sunny July.
Gun fun.
Trump, trump,
U.S. slumps.
                    Such fun?

U.S. rum-drunk,
burnt.
                    Such fun?
Ruckus hungry.
Rumpus thump. Much pull-push.
Guns fuck us up.
Trump fucks us up.

                    Shut up, shut up.
Run.
                    Such fun?

Skull hurts,
syrup s p u r t   s,
lungs full,
mucus,
pus,
sputum.

Upchuck.

Drugs' dull *drum drum* thud.
                    Such fun?

U.S. just burnt fungus.
Ugly, ugly.

Truth, but mustn't fuss.
Hush, hush.

                Such fun?
                Such fun?

Sunny July.
Guns.
Trump.
U.S.

STORY OF OLD JOHN

Robyn Hood spots Old John on rob, blows horn.

ROBYN HOOD
Old John, stop! Folly!

OLD JOHN
(Old John drops books)
Oof! Stop?

ROBYN HOOD
Don't rob poor. Not good, old John. Not good.

OLD JOHN
Old John's not, Robyn.

ROBYN HOOD
Old John's got monks' books. Monks poor, John, monks
poor.

OLD JOHN
Not, Robyn. Monks go to school. So not poor.

ROBYN HOOD
Monks do go to school … So?

OLD JOHN
Monks posh.

ROBYN HOOD
Monks not posh, John.

OLD JOHN
Monks own books, so posh.

ROBYN HOOD
Monk's not posh, John. Monks lowly.

OLD JOHN
Monks not lowly – own books. Old John's not got books.

ROBYN HOOD
Monks own books, not got food or goods.

OLD JOHN
Monks own books. Books sold for food.

ROBYN HOOD
No, John. Don't rob monks. Monks poor.

OLD JOHN
Poppycock Robyn, Monks posh, got God.

ROBYN HOOD
God's poor, John.

OLD JOHN
Poppycock … God's not poor!

ROBYN HOOD
God's poor – good book shows so.

OLD JOHN
Poppycock, God's got gold. Monks don gold cross.

ROBYN HOOD
Monks only borrow gold cross from God.

OLD JOHN
So, John borrow God's cross from monks for food!

ROBYN HOOD
No. Not good.

OLD JOHN
No?

ROBYN HOOD
No, no, don't rob God, John. Not good.

OLD JOHN
Not good. How?

ROBYN HOOD
God's got control of holy crown, or ... down, down.

OLD JOHN
Oh! Old John not know. Sorry.

ROBYN HOOD
Don't worry.

OLD JOHN
Old John's sorry.

ROBYN HOOD
Good.

OLD JOHN
Who Old John rob now?

ROBYN HOOD
Lords, John.

OLD JOHN
How Old John know Lords?

ROBYN HOOD
Lords from London; bozos who hold swords.

OLD JOHN
Oh ... Monk Rollo's from London, so ...

ROBYN HOOD
Poppycock.

OLD JOHN
Not poppycock, Robyn. Rollo's from Croydon.

ROBYN HOOD
(Robyn yowls)
DO NOT ROB MONKS OR GOD!

OLD JOHN
Oh no! Old John's got Robyn cross.
(Old John sobs forlornly)

ROBYN HOOD
No. Robyn's not cross.

OLD JOHN
Not?

ROBYN HOOD
No … Now Old John knows to only rob Lords.

OLD JOHN
Only Lords who hold swords from London.

ROBYN HOOD
Gold swords, Old John.

OLD JOHN
(Old John broods)
Robyn's got gold sword … Robyn's from London?

ROBYN HOOD
Robyn's from North Notts' woods.

OLD JOHN
North Notts, not London?

ROBYN HOOD
No, no, not London.

OLD JOHN
Robyn Hood's Lord?

ROBYN HOOD
Sort of, long story.

OLD JOHN
Oh do go on, Robyn.

ROBYN HOOD
Robyn Hood, son of Lord.

OLD JOHN
So, Lord Robyn Hood?

ROBYN HOOD
No, Robyn's not Lord.
(*Old John looks on gold sword*)
Stop, stop fool!

OLD JOHN
Old John no fool, gold swords sold for corn.

ROBYN HOOD
No, no …
(*Old John robs Robyn of blood*)

OLD JOHN
No holy crown for Old John now, only down, down …

BUNBURY

Bunbury spurns truth,
churns up muck,
hurts us.

Mustn't trust Bunbury,
flub-duh-dub Bunbury.
Humbug.

#
(For Andrew Tate)

#Andy's a man,
an alpha, angry, man's man,
a card shark.
Says *"Stay away Mr Tax Man."*

Andy's all lads' mags,
mayhap,
fast cars,
party and bars.

Andy has antsy pants bants,
a wank a day,
slaps slags away.
"Spank, spank!
#gangbang,"
says Andy.

Andy hangs lads' mags as art,
farts manly,
calls Lady Gaga a fat tart.

#alpha
#twat

Bon Mots

Knock. Knock.
Who knocks?
Doctor.
Doctor who?
Doctor Who owns show.
Horror of Lost Zygons.
Not good bon mot.
Doctor Who got tools.
Stop now fool.
Oh.

Knock. Knock.
Who knocks?
Doctor.
Doctor who?
Doctor dot.
Doctor dot who?
Forgot – lost for words.
Not good bon mot.
Dot to dot shows cow.
Stop now.
Oh, ok.

Henry VIII

Leeches bleed me.

She,
green sleeves. She,
bejewelled, breeds,
then severed neck bleeds.

Leeches bleed me.

TAJ MAHAL

```
S Y G Q K R H C S L L A H A
Y H A L L A H A L L A I G S
A Y E S A A T S Y D U A R Y
W C A V N S O H U D S B A I
L N A T P N S A R T A R M G
A S A O S V R H K Q P L A A
T T T M C O V J S W H J L S
F S W A R D D A A A V B A P
S A N D J N G H M L A H S N
T B Q R A M N A A L G W I A
P A I L E C A N D S R Z S S
D R A F T S S H G B A K Y Z
M Y M A R Y A M A R S A I U
T N A R G A R F T L D O I D
```

~~Pray~~	~~at~~	Taj Mahal	Agra
Chant	Allah Allah	~~at~~	~~Taj Mahal~~
Say	Salam	~~at~~	~~Taj Mahal~~
~~A~~ land	sand	~~and~~	glass
Gasp ~~at~~	~~Taj Mahal's~~	vast	halls
Man	sang	saga ~~at~~	~~Taj Mahal~~
Shah Jahan	asks	fragrant	~~lady~~
Stay	~~Stay~~	always	~~at~~
~~Taj Mahal~~	Days	~~and~~	~~days~~
~~Shah Jahan~~	drafts	walls	~~as~~ art
Draws	~~fragrant~~	lady	~~as~~
damask	~~Pray~~	~~pray~~	pray
~~at~~	~~Taj Mahal~~	My Maryam	~~My Maryam~~

I'm in sick mind clinic. I'm girl hiding. I'm sphinx bird.
I'm myth. Hybrid misfit bitch. This is shit! This is shit.
I fit in with it, this shit clinic! This filthy, dingy bin!
 Things fling fists with wind,
 fight, fight, kick shins, thighs.
 Hit, hit!

I'm girl hiding, hiding.
 My mind sick within.
 I'm fifty-fifty witch,
 fifty-fifty victim.
Bind my iris wings with rigid wrists.
 Grip tightly,
 I'm spinning …
 Grip tightly.
I'm tricky. I'm mind sick. I will rid this sin-skin,
this itching, bitching skin I'm in. I'm mind sick.
This kitsch thinking is nihilism.
I'm sphinx bird in flight. Divinity is cynicism.

I'm fighting, bristling with hiss.
I stick pins in skin, in thick thighs …
 Spinning, I cry.
 I'm mind sick.
 "Is it midnight?"

Shitty hybrid bird in bits, twitching with indignity.
 Spinning,
 spinning.

Bright lights.
Him. It. It …
In scripts it's writ: *Bring Pink Pills*.
Fly Sphinx bird fly high.
>Swirling,
>whirling,
>twirling,
>twisting,
>girlishly flirting with light.

I'm mind sick.
My shrink stings with his criticism.
His simplistic thinking.
His witticism, his glib tips.

This sphinx bird girl is dying, dying.
Sphinx bird is dying, lying, crying in dirt.
>Sighing,
>sighing,
>crying
>*"Is it midnight?"*

Spirits lift with first light …
Writ in pink pill bliss …

>Sphinx bird rising.
>I'm still I.

WAYLAND SMASHY

That was a black day.
Wayland's way was a dark, dark path.
Alas, man falls at chalk wall.
"Hard, hard," says Wayland Smashy.
"What a man was, acts as man's past."
A backwards start.

A sham backwards start.
That damp, dark May Day
acts as man's past.
A hard and marshland path.
"Harsh, harsh," says Wayland Smashy,
as man falls fast at chalk wall.

Man falls at chalk wall,
a backwards start.
"Harsh, harsh," says Wayland Smashy.
"That was a black day."
A chalky and grassy path.
What a man was, acts as man's past.

What a man was, acts as man's past,
as man sat sad at tall chalk wall.
A dark and marshy path.
A flat day.
A backwards start.
"Hard, hard," says Wayland Smashy.

"A dark walk," says Wayland Smashy.
"What a man casts, acts as man's past."

A day. A day
sad man gawks at hard chalk wall.
A hard start,
that dark and wayward path.

"Harsh, harsh," says Wayland Smashy.
A day. A day
a calm path
man shall start.
Wayland Smashy crafts a way past wall,
says: *"What a man was, acts as man's past."*

That last black day was a happy day.
Man has a way past wall.
What a man was, acts as man's past.

FISH 'N' TRIP

Int. Night.
Ritz. Bright lights.

KIKI
(Shyly)
Is it Sid?

SID
Hi bird. Girl is fit, innit. Killing it with kinky bikini pics.
(Sid winks)
I'd hit it.

KIKI
It? It? … Think this is wit? Sigh.
(Kiki twists with grit)

SID
Bir— Kiki, ting is, I'm fishing … Fishing … Thirsty?

KIKI
Nix. Sid is tripping.

SID
Trip?
(Sid thinks)
Kiki? Drink? Pint? Fizzy gin? Sniff? Pills?

KIKI
Pills? Sigh. First instinct is grim. I'm splitting, Sid.

SID
Right … Think, think … … … Picnic?

KIKI

Picnic?

SID

With crisps?

KIKI

(Kiki grins)

Picnic it is.

SID

Sit, Kiki, sit. I'll sing …

(Sid sings)

"Wild thing, I think I …"

KIKI

I … I … Sigh!

SID

Kiki, sit, I insist.

KIKI

Why?

SID

Big dick. Six-inch, innit.

KIKI

Child! Sigh.

SID

Kiss?

KIKI

(Kiki clicks digits)

Dismiss.

SID

Chill … It's fishing, innit. Sit.

KIKI
I think ick.

SID
(*Sid slyly slips pill in Kiki's drink*)
Drink?

KIKI
I think nix.
(*Kiki flicks wrists*)

SID
Sit, Kiki, sit. I'm kind … I'm kind … Bit thick … Bit victim …

KIKI
Victim? Why?

SID
Sit, Kiki, sit. Shy, skinny kid with thick bin-lids, hit with fists.

KIKI
(*Kiki sits shyly*)
Spill?

SID
Chill! Drink! I'm thinking.

KIKI
(*Kiki sips*)
Is this gin?

SID
Drink minx.
(*Kiki drinks*)
Night's lit?

KIKI
It's middling, I think.

SID

Middling, right, right. Drink, drink, Kiki. Finish it.

KIKI

(Kiki drinks)

Sid? Why Ritz? Bit shit, bit dingy ... Films? ... Why films? ...
I ... I ... Sid, is it bit? ... Bit thingy? ... Tingling ...

SID

Fish is biting ... Ting is, bird's lipstick, bird's tight shirt,
skimpy skirt, big tits is ... Sid's trick, innit.

KIKI

Trick? ... Sid, I'm dizzy ...

SID

Kiss?

KIKI

Nix ... Nix!

SID

Frigid bitch.
(Sid hiss, hits Kiki)

KIKI

(Kiki sickly spins)

Sid ... I'm sick ... I'm bird flying, flying.
(Kiki's rising, rising)

SID

Fly, my bird, fly.

KIKI

I'm flying, flying. I'm bird, Sid, bird.
(Kiki's limbs lift in flight)

SID

Dizzy bitch. Kiss?

KIKI

Dis—

SID

Silly bitch, why fight it? Sir Sid is Kiki's fright-knight …
Kiki's kiss?

KIKI

Kiki is hiding, Sid.

SID

I will find … Pink lips, hips, thick thighs, big tits. Bird.
My bird.

KIKI

I'm flying in sky, Sid. Find, find?
(Kiki thinks; flirting, lifts skirt)

SID

(Sid licks lips, drinks drink)
Dick's stiff.

KIKI

Sid's dick is gift … Bind it with pink string, bring, bring …
"Wild thing, I think I … I think I …"

SID

(Sid's rising, rising)
Kiki …
(Kiki twirls, kicking Sid's shins; Sid slips)
Bitch! Why?

KIKI

(Kiki impishly grins)
My Kiki trick.

SID
Witch.

KIKI
Sid, I'm bird. Bird … Ting is Sid, this girl is myth, innit …
(Kiki clicks digits)
Dismiss … Dismiss.

(Midnight finds Sid crying in pink pill trip)

BANKSY

Ban Banksy!
Ban vandal's trashy art!
A scandal as Banksy's spray-cans fart anarchy;
blatantly attacks law and cash.
Bananas as *bang bang* span walls and canvas.
Ants, cats and *gangsta* rats.

Daft abstract?

Chants sang as angry mass asks *what?*
What?

Flags at half-mast as Banksy starts class war.

       Abracadabra:
       napalm.

Ban Banksy!

The Seven Elves

Seven teeny-weeny men
dwelled between cemetery bells.
Seven teeny-weeny men held
three fermented fennel seeds.

Sleepy severely needs bedrest;
seeks helter-shelter.
Testy gets vexed by Sleepy's weed-dependence;
seems senseless.

Sneezy smells the breeze,
the elements spell he rendered.
Three fermented fennel seeds,
blended well.

The eldest, well-esteemed Mender elf, lends temper:
"Let Sleepy be, let Sleepy be."

Gentle Glee: blessed, yet newly stressed
(he recklessly spends the rent).

Reserved, the chef, fetches
fresh nettles, nest-eggs, beef, red bell peppers, shells, jelly.
Serves refreshments.

Less-Clever feels perplexed by spells.
He's the beekeeper.
Bees less fervent, less edgy.
Seven men.

Sneezy smells the breeze.
Three fermented fennel seeds.

LAST MACDARAGH HAD A FARM

Last Macdaragh had a farm, B.C.G.A. [4]
And that farm had a namby pamby lamb –
a baa-baa ta dah and a baa-baa ta that,
Last Macdaragh had a farm, B.C.G.A.

And that farm had a barmy llama –
a wah-wah-waahh and a wah-wah ta that,
and a baa-baa ta dah, a baa-baa ta that,
Last Macdaragh had a farm, B.C.G.A.

And that farm had an awkward cat –
a scratch-scratch ta dah and a scratch-scratch ta that,
a wah-wah-waahh, a wah-wah ta that,
a baa-baa ta dah, a baa-baa ta that,
Last Macdaragh had a farm, B.C.G.A.

And that farm had an angry calf –
a stamp-stamp ta dah and a stamp-stamp ta that,
a scratch-scratch ta dah, a scratch-scratch ta that,
a wah-wah-waahh, a wah-wah ta that,
a baa-baa ta dah, a baa-baa ta that,
Last Macdaragh had a farm, B.C.G.A.

And that farm had a happy alpaca –
a clap-clap ta dah and a clap-clap ta that,
a stamp-stamp ta dah, a stamp-stamp ta that,
a scratch-scratch ta dah, a scratch-scratch ta that,
a wah-wah-waahh, a wah-wah ta that,
a baa-baa ta dah, a baa-baa ta that,
Last Macdaragh had a farm, B.C.G.A.

And that farm had handy randy ram –
a bam-bam ta dah and a bam-bam ta that,
a clap-clap ta dah, a clap-clap ta that,
a stamp-stamp ta dah, a stamp-stamp ta that,
a scratch-scratch ta dah, a scratch-scratch ta that,
a wah-wah-waahh, a wah-wah ta that,
a baa-baa ta dah, a baa-baa ta that,
Last Macdaragh had a farm, B.C.G.A.

And that farm had a barn, a thatch hatch, a yard, a dam, land
… and gas!
A cash wad ta dah and a cash wad ta that
and abracadabra,
blah, blah, blah,
Last Macdaragh has a flat, B.C.G.A.

---

[4] B.C.G.A. is the acronym of the British Compressed Gases Association.

ROBOTS

Robots do not grow old,
only worn down.

SAKANA

Japan has Tankas.
Apt and small katakana.
Start: a sakana.
A man that can, can Tanka.
A lady thanks – may marry.

USUFRUCT

Dutch fun, but funky.

Dutch buy surplus truckfuls –
lucky ducks –
but usufruct study.

Dutch guy dumbstruck.
Fluffy duck dunts lucht,
thump, thump, thump.

Un-duck.

But un-duck unlucky –
Tufty duck fully fucks fluffy un-duck –
kus, kus.

Dutch guy hung up un-duck
'kunst'.

Dutch fun, but funky.[5]

---

[5] Dead Duck Day, as if you didn't already know, is celebrated annually on 5th June outside the Natural History Museum in Rotterdam, Netherlands. It commemorates the day one of its researchers made an Ig Nobel prize-winning discovery: the first recorded description of homosexual necrophilia in ducks.

Samantha calls Tracy a *slarg-ag*.
"*What?!*" says Tracy.
Samantha barbs, "*Wharg-at?*"
"*What, what?!*" says Tracy?
Samantha ha-ha's, "*Carg-an
yarg-a targ-alks argy-bargy?*"
"*What, what?!*" says Tracy?
Samantha ha-ha's.

Tracy slaps Samantha.
Samantha slaps Tracy back.

A thwack-whack-crack abacas attack.
An argy-bargy.

Maths staff bans all argy-bargy chat.
Sacks Mr Black.

HOROLOGY

Horology –
work on clocks.
Tock, tock, tock,
on, off, on, off.

Chronos cross,
lost flow of now.
Logbooks shows onyx block.
Stop, stop, stop!

GIGI

Gigi is child,
flighty high-spirits child,
ditsy chick in pink frills,
sickly singing ditty,
"Tiny girls, tiny girls."

Bit sick, isn't it?

Gigi, still child,
girlishly flirts with Mr Big.
Mr Big is thirty-six,
stylishly priggish rich,
high-flying bigwig.

Bit sick, isn't it?

Bit disinhibiting,
him dismissing Gigi.
Childish whimsy.
Mr Big is filthy in his thinking.
Mr Big living in skirt-swinging sin,
illicit trysts with girls swilling gin,
him whining in ink

whilst Gigi's crying,
"It is him,
it is him."
This isn't childish whimsy.
This is it. This is it.

Gigi drinks gin.
Bit sick, isn't it?

In Spring, Mr Big visits Gigi.
Gigi chic in lipstick,
slinky, silk slip,
bright lights shining midnight.
Hmmm thinks Mr Big illicitly,
glimpsing virgin's tight skin, thighs,
thin midriff, tiny hips.
Mr Big licks his lips.

Bit sick, isn't it?

Mr Big insists Gigi's gift is sin,
his whim, his sixth wish.
Gigi fights with him.
This visit is grim.
Mr Big flits in hissing fit,
Gigi's grizzling,
still singing.
Still bit sick, isn't it?

Mr Big, missing Gigi,
brings Gigi ring.
Gigi's first frisky kiss with him.
Gigi wins him.
Finish with singing.

ODD SOCKS

Two months of box of frogs,
odd socks,
locks on locks on locks,
cross lost words of *no, no,*
yo-yo moods.
Box of frogs,
rocky stop stops,
books on storms,
hooks of *sorry, sorry,*
sob, sob,
no control.
Cold cloths of foggy
moth cocoons.

Two months.
No snowdrops bloom.
Box of frogs.

Not for tomorrow.
For two months only.

Sorry
not
sorry.

NYMPHS

Thy chyld fynds blyss
wyth bryght lyghts,
nyght sky lyt wyth wyld nymphs.

Shss shss,
wyth nymphs' kynd kyss
thy chyld fynds blyss.

EUPHORIA

A day.
Pagan May plays,
prays at altar and dark arts at dawn.

Shy buds unfurl.
July: sunburnt, shuns hurly-burly.

September remembers seeds sewn,
evergreen, evergreen.

Months follow months,
old, so old.

Idyllic bliss in living.
Idyllic bliss in
euphoria.

```
S Y G Q K R H C S L L A H A
Y H A L L A H A L L A I G S
A Y E S A A T S Y D U A R Y
W C A V N S O H U D S B A I
L N A T P N S A R T A R M G
A S A O S V R H K Q P L A A
T T T M C O V J S W H J L S
F S W A R D D A A A V B A P
S A N D J N G H M L A H S N
T B Q R A M N A A L G W I A
P A I L E C A N D S R Z S S
D R A F T S S H G B A K Y Z
M Y M A R Y A M A R S A I U
T N A R G A R F T L D O I D
```